Helen,
Sometimes I think
you are under more
pressure than you
admit so when I saw
this I thought of you.
All my love.
x Fiona x

Let It Be

Prayers, poems and
scriptures for those
under pressure
Illustrated by Lyn Ellis

Kevin
Mayhew

First published in Great Britain in 1994 by
KEVIN MAYHEW LTD
Rattlesden
Bury St Edmunds
Suffolk IP30 0SZ

ISBN 0 86209 469 0

© 1994 Kevin Mayhew Limited

Printed in Hong Kong
by Colorcraft

Contents

	Page
Deep Peace	5
His Love	5
Let Me Be	6
Leisure	8
Paul's Farewell	10
God of Time	11
Kitchen Prayer	12
The Peace of God	13
When You're Lonely	14
Bless our Home	15
Lord, Your Way is Perfect	16
Safe in God's Keeping	17
Do Not Be Afraid	18
When Dreams are Broken	19
The Lord Our Protector	20
A Prayer When Distracted	22
Remind Me, Lord	24
Be at Peace	25
Never Too Busy To Care	26
God Has Not Promised	27
I Asked Jesus	28
Peace	29

Give Me Patience	30
God Grant Me Serenity	31
The Twenty-Third Psalm	32
I am convinced	34
The Lord is my rock	35
Take Time	36
The Difference	38
On His Blindness	40
The Lord of hosts	42
The fruit of the Spirit	42
Though the fig tree	43
Be still	43
Give Me Time	44
A Prayer for Patience	45
Two Marys	46
Together	47
Safe Through the Night	48

Deep Peace

Deep peace of the Running Wave to you.
Deep peace of the Flowing Air to you.
Deep peace of the Quiet Earth to you.
Deep peace of the Shining Stars to you.
Deep peace of the Son of Peace to you.

His Love

May his love enfold you.
May his peace surround you.
May his light touch you.

Let Me Be

God,
let me be.
Let me not rush, and worry,
let me not think continuously,
anxiously,
about tomorrow.
Let me enjoy today.

Let me be.
Let me not seek always to justify
myself by achievement.
Let me not exhaust myself
and others by chasing success.

Let me enjoy your
unconditional love.

Let me be.
Let me not turn to work to avoid
facing myself.
Let me not use noisy activity to
drown the whisper of your voice.
Let me be still.

Let me be.

MICHAEL FORSTER

Leisure

What is this life if,
full of care,
we have no time
to stand and stare?

No time to stand beneath
the boughs
and stare as long as sheep or cows.

No time to see,
when woods we pass,
where squirrels hide
their nuts in grass.

No time to see, in broad daylight,
streams full of stars,
like skies at night.

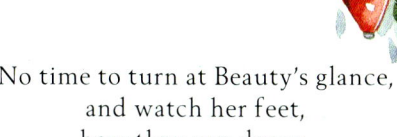

No time to turn at Beauty's glance,
and watch her feet,
how they can dance.

No time to wait till her mouth can
enrich that smile
her eyes began?

A poor life this if,
full of care,
we have no time to stand and stare.

WILLIAM HENRY DAVIES

Paul's Farewell

Be happy
and grow in Christ.

Do what I have said,
and live in harmony
and peace.

May the grace of our Lord
Jesus Christ
be with you all.

May God's love,
and the Holy Spirit's
friendship,
be yours.

2 Corinthians 13:11-14

God of Time

You are the God of time.
Why is there so little of it?
Why don't you give me more?
I could use it,
spend it,
occupy it,
fill it.
It wouldn't matter how much
you gave me.
It would always be full.
There would never be enough.

Don't give me any more.
Teach me to enjoy what there is.
Be the God of time.
Be the God of *my* time.

MICHAEL FORSTER

Kitchen Prayer

Lord of pots and pans and things,
since I've not the time to be a saint
by doing lovely things,
or watching late with thee,
or dreaming in the dawn light,
or storming heaven's gates,
make me a saint by getting meals
and washing up the plates.
Although I must have
Martha's hands,
I have a Mary mind,
and when I black the boots and shoes
thy sandals, Lord, I find.
I think of how they trod the earth
what time I scrub the floor;
accept this meditation, Lord,
I haven't time for more.

The Peace of God

Have no anxiety about anything
but in everything,
by prayer and supplication,
with thanksgiving, let your requests
be made known to God.

And the peace of God,
which passes all understanding,
will keep your hearts
and your minds
in Christ Jesus.

Philippians 4:4-7

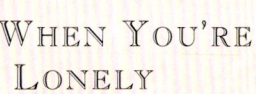

WHEN YOU'RE LONELY

When you're lonely,
I wish you love.

When you're down,
I wish you joy.

When you're troubled,
I wish you peace.

When things are complicated,
I wish you simple beauty.

When things look empty,
I wish you hope.

Bless our Home

Bless our home, Father,
that we cherish the bread
before there is none,
discover each other
before we leave,
and enjoy each other
for what we are,
while we have time.

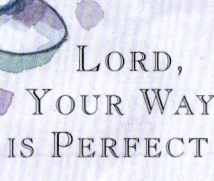

Lord, Your Way is Perfect

Lord, your way
is perfect:
help us always to trust
in your goodness,
so that, walking with you
and following you
in all simplicity,
we may possess
quiet and contented minds,
and may cast all our care
on you,
for you care for us.
Grant this, Lord,
for your dear Son's sake,
Jesus Christ.

Safe in God's Keeping

Look at the sparrows
so small and light,
not one is forgotten
in God's sight.

So rejoice in his love
and take delight.
You are worth more
than hundreds of sparrows.

Matthew 10:31

Do Not Be Afraid

Do not be afraid,
for I have redeemed you.
I have called you by your name;
you are mine.

When you walk through
the waters, I'll be with you;
you will never sink
beneath the waves.
When the fear of loneliness
is looming,
then remember
I am at your side.
You are mine, O my child,
I am your Father,
and I love you
with a perfect love.

BASED ON ISAIAH 43 1-5

When Dreams are Broken

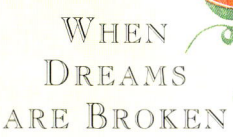

When dreams are broken things
and joy has fled,
there is Jesus.
When hope is a struggle
and faith a fragile thread,
there is Jesus.

When grief is a shadow
and peace unknown,
there is Jesus.
When we need the assurance
that we're not alone,
there is Jesus.

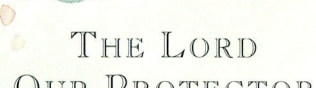

THE LORD
OUR PROTECTOR

I lift up my eyes to the hills.
From whence does my help come?
My help comes from the Lord,
who made heaven and earth.

He will not let your foot be moved,
he who keeps you will not slumber.
Behold, he who keeps Israel
will neither slumber nor sleep.

The Lord is your keeper;
the Lord is your shade on
your right hand.
The sun shall not smite you by day,
nor the moon by night.

The Lord will keep you from all evil;
he will keep your life.
The Lord will keep your going out
and your coming in,
from this time forth
and for evermore.

PSALM 121

A Prayer When Distracted

When the heart is hard
and parched up
come upon me with a shower
of mercy.
When grace is lost from life
come with a burst of song.
When tumultuous work
raises its din on all sides,
shutting me out from beyond,

come to me,
my Lord of silence,
with thy peace and rest.
When my beggarly heart
sits crouched,
shut up in a corner,
break open the door
and come with the ceremony
of a king.
When desire blinds the mind
with delusion and dust,
O thou holy one, thou wakeful,
come with thy light
and thy thunder.

REMIND ME, LORD

Remind me, Lord, that your love
is bigger than any problem.
The more I look at the problem,
the bigger the problem becomes.
But when I look to you, Lord,
my anxiety pales
in the light of your love.

Be at Peace

Do not look forward
to what might happen tomorrow;
the same everlasting Father
who cares for you today
will take care of you
tomorrow and every day.
Be at peace, then,
and put aside
all anxious thoughts
and imaginings.

Francis de Sales

NEVER TOO BUSY TO CARE

Lord, make me so sensitive
to the needs of those around me
that I never fail to know
when they're hurting or afraid;
or when they're simply crying out
for someone's touch
to ease their loneliness.
Let me love so much that my
first thought is of others
and my last thought is of me.

God Has Not Promised

God has not promised
sun without rain,
joy without sorrow,
peace without pain.
But God has promised
strength for the day,
rest for the labour,
light for the way,
grace for the trials,
help from above,
unfailing sympathy,
undying love.

I Asked Jesus

I asked
Jesus
'How much do
you love me?'
'This much,'
he answered, and
he stretched out
his arms and died.

Peace

Lead me from death to life,
from falsehood to truth;
lead me from despair to hope,
from fear to trust.

Lead me from hate to love,
from war to peace;
let your peace fill our hearts,
our lives and our world.

Give Me Patience

It isn't in the quiet,
in the solitude of the study,
that I grow, Lord,
rather at the
supermarket checkout
or behind a
hopeless traffic jam.
Give me the deep
breath of calm
when the clock is racing.

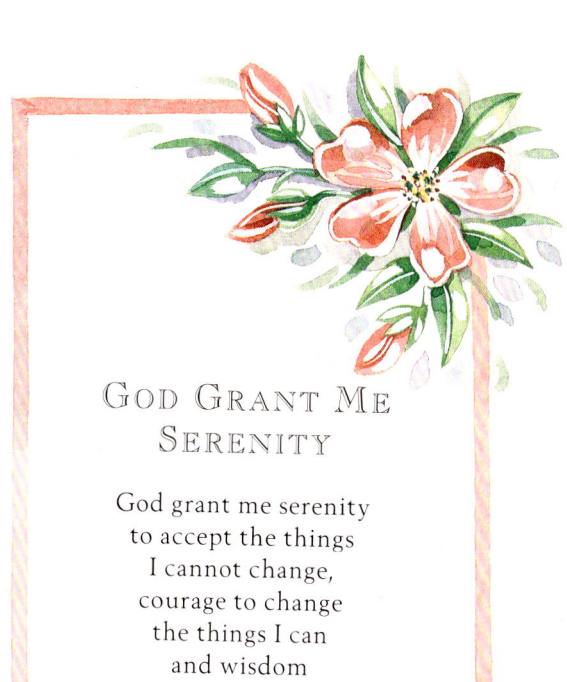

God Grant Me Serenity

God grant me serenity
to accept the things
I cannot change,
courage to change
the things I can
and wisdom
to know the difference.

The Twenty-Third Psalm

The Lord is my shepherd,
I shall not want.
He makes me lie down
in green pastures.
He leads me
beside still waters;
he restores my soul.

He guides me in
paths of righteousness
for his name's sake.
Even though I walk through

the valley of the
shadow of death,
I fear no evil;
for you are with me;
your rod and
your staff comfort me.
You prepare a table before me
in the presence of my enemies.
You anoint my head with oil.
My cup overflows.
Surely goodness and love
shall follow me
all the days of my life.
And I shall live
in the house of the Lord
for ever.

I am convinced that
neither death, nor life,
nor angels, nor rulers,
nor things present,
nor things to come,
nor powers, nor height,
nor depth, nor anything else
in all creation,
will be able to separate us
from the love of God
in Christ Jesus our Lord.

ROMANS 8:38-39

The Lord is my rock,
my fortress,
and my deliverer,
my God, my rock
in whom I take refuge,
my shield,
and the horn of my salvation,
my stronghold.

Psalm 18:2

Take Time

Take time to THINK ...
it is the source of power.
Take time to PLAY ...
it is the secret of perpetual youth.
Take time to READ ...
it is the fountain of wisdom.
Take time to PRAY ...
it is the greatest power on earth.
Take time to LOVE
and BE LOVED ...
it is a God-given privilege.

Take time to BE FRIENDLY . . .
it is the road to happiness.
Take time to LAUGH . . .
it is the music of the soul.
Take time to GIVE . . .
it is too short a day to be selfish.
Take time to WORK . . .
it is the price of success.
Take time to DO CHARITY . . .
it is the key to heaven.

The Difference

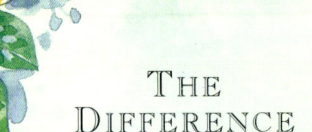

I got up early one morning and
rushed right into the day;
I had so much to accomplish that
I didn't have time to pray.
Problems just tumbled about me,
and heavier came each task.
'Why doesn't God help me?'
I wondered,
he answered, 'You didn't ask.'

I wanted to see joy and beauty,
but the day toiled on grey and bleak,
I wondered why God
didn't show me;
he said, 'You didn't seek.'
I tried to come into God's presence;
I used all my keys at the lock.
God gently and lovingly chided,
'My child, you didn't knock'.

I woke up early this morning,
and paused before entering the day;
I had so much to accomplish
that I had to take time to pray.

On His Blindness

When I consider
how my light is spent,
ere half my days,
in this dark world and wide,
and that one talent
which is death to hide,
lodged with me useless,
though my soul more bent
to serve therewith my maker,
and present
my true account,
lest he returning chide,
'Doth God exact day-labour,
light denied?'

I fondly ask.
But patience, to prevent
that murmur, soon replies,
'God doth not need either
man's work or his own gifts;
who best bear his mild yoke,
they serve him best.
His state is kingly:
thousands at his bidding speed,
and post o'er land and ocean
without rest;
they also serve who only
stand and wait.'

JOHN MILTON

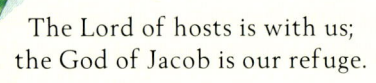

The Lord of hosts is with us;
the God of Jacob is our refuge.

PSALM 46:11

The fruit of the Spirit is love,
joy, peace, gentleness, goodness,
faith, meekness, temperance.

GALATIANS 5:22-23

Though the fig tree does not blossom, and no fruit is on the vines; though the produce of the olive fails and the fields yield no food; though the flock is cut off from the fold and there is no herd in the stalls, yet I will rejoice in the Lord; I will exult in the God of my salvation.

Habakkuk 3:17:18

Be still, and know
that I am God.

Psalm 46:10

GIVE ME TIME

God,
give me time.
So much to do;
people to impress,
time to exploit.
I have to justify my existence.

God,
give me time.
Change my perspective.
Teach me to value people,
not impress them.
Teach me to value time,
not exploit it.
Teach me to value myself.

God,
give me time.

A Prayer for Patience

When my patience
seems too short
help me stretch it;
teach me how to meet
a crisis with a smile.
When I'm running out
of quick and clever answers
let the questions stop
for just a little while.

When it seems as though
the day has too few hours
in which to do the things
I have to do,
may I always find the time
for what's important –
time for listening,
time for love
and laughter too.

Two Marys

The Lord answered her, 'Martha, Martha, you are worried and distracted by many things; there is need of only one thing. Mary has chosen the better part, which will not be taken away from her.'

Luke 10:41-42

Then Mary said, 'Here am I, the servant of the Lord; let it be with me according to your word.' Then the angel departed from her.

Luke 1:38

Together

Lord, help me remember
that nothing
is going to happen today
that you and I
cannot handle together.

SAFE THROUGH THE NIGHT

Now I lay me down to sleep
I pray the Lord my soul to keep,
and keep me safe
throughout the night,
and wake me
with the morning light.

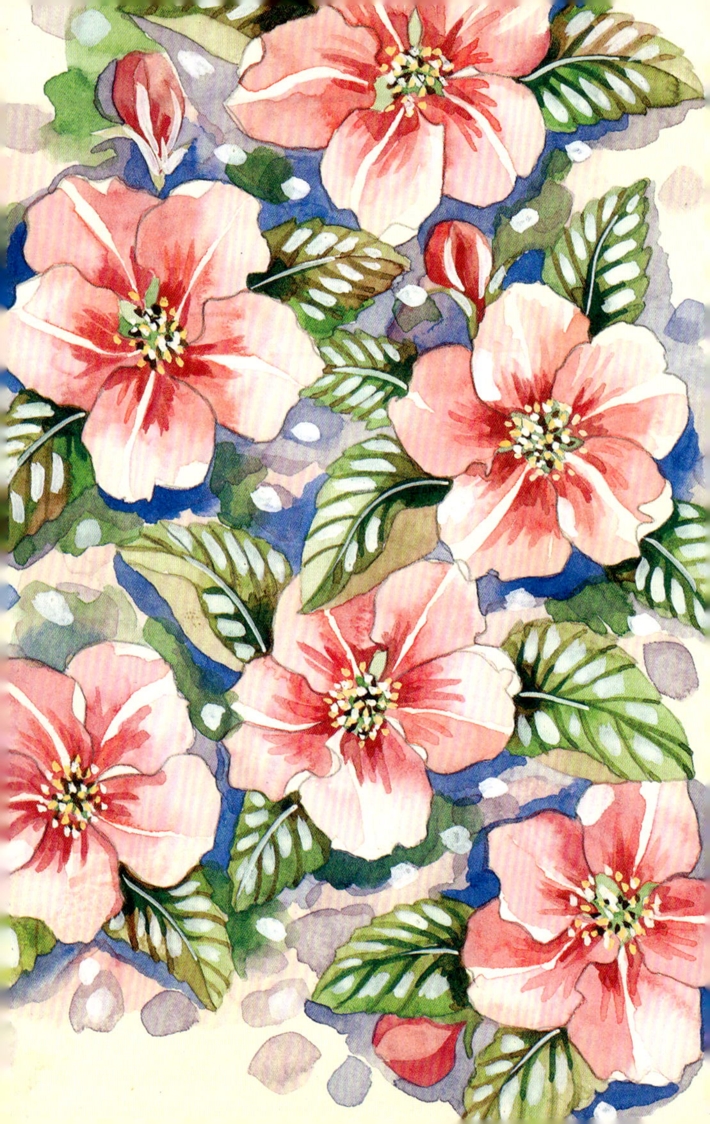